You Can Learn
Sign Language!

More than 300 Words in Pictures

Jackie Kramer & Tali Ovadia

Troll

Dedication

For Stuart, who listens with his heart.
— Jackie

For Victor, another Show of Hands.
— with love, Tali

Dear Reader:

As a Deaf educational psychologist working with deaf children and their families, and as a Deaf Studies instructor, I am often asked to recommend American Sign Language (ASL) books for young children, both deaf and hearing. Unfortunately, I have found only a few ASL books and no dictionaries suitable for deaf children.

You Can Learn Sign Language! is a welcome addition to the list of quality ASL books for deaf and hearing children currently available. This dictionary is unique, in that the authors involved deaf and hearing children plus consultants who are deaf in planning and developing the book. *You Can Learn Sign Language!* is an educational and engaging introduction to an often overlooked but very important American language, American Sign Language.

Edward Ingham, Ph.D.
Portland, Oregon

Acknowledgments:
Ivette Bellanca, Shauna Bilyeu and Edward Ingham

Many thanks to our signers:

Emma Bardagjy   **Ashley Butcher**   **Akram Hakkoum**   **Colton Knudsen**   **Kevin Perkins**

Text copyright © 1999 by Jackie Kramer and Tali Ovadia.
Illustrations copyright © 1999 by John Smith.
Photographs copyright © 1999 by Alan Butcher/Butcher Photographic.

Published by Troll Communications L.L.C.

You Can Learn Sign Language! is produced by becker&mayer!, Kirkland, Washington.
www.beckermayer.com

Design by Heidi Baughman
Edited by Stephanie Westcott and Jennifer Worick

Printed in the United States of America. ISBN 0-8167-6336-4
10 9 8 7 6 5 4 3 2

Contents

Welcome to American Sign Language!

hello

Deaf people around the world speak many different languages. Here in the United States, American Sign Language, or ASL, evolved when American deaf people wanted to communicate with one another. Many people believe wrongly that ASL is simply English "spoken" with the hands. Although there are other American sign communication systems that *are* word-for-word translations of spoken English into signs, only ASL is a true language.

As a language, ASL is always expanding to keep pace with our ever-changing world. ASL has slang expressions, word-play and even "accents" or dialects depending on which part of the country the signer is from. And as new technology or discoveries are made, new words are added to the ASL vocabulary.

Like any language, ASL has its own rules, word order, and grammar. These may seem confusing or difficult at first. But once you've had a little practice, ASL is easy! Here are a few things you need to know before you get started:

no
Make a mouth with your first two fingers and your thumb. Now open and close it!

A Case of Space

Imagine a rectangle that reaches from the top of your head to your waist and from one shoulder to the other. This is your signing space. It's important to keep your hands in this area of your body while signing so the person watching you can see your signs clearly. Whenever possible, sign in the direction of the person you are talking to, and remember not to block the view of any other signers.

not
Flick your thumb out and away from your chin.

Getting Negative

Adding a "not" or "no" sign to a sentence usually makes it negative. Negative sentences are also created by making negative head movements and expressions while signing the sentence.

Mind Your Manners!

It's important to be polite when using ASL or any language. Try some of these, please!

sorry
Rotate your fist over your heart.

thank you
Put your fingers to your mouth and then move your hand straight out in front of you.

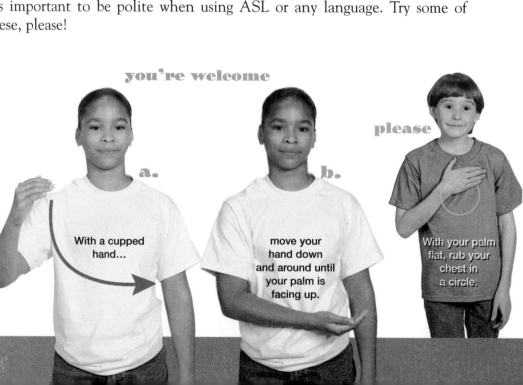

you're welcome

a.
With a cupped hand...

b.
move your hand down and around until your palm is facing up.

please
With your palm flat, rub your chest in a circle.

Excuse Me

If two people are signing and you need to get by, you can walk through the conversation. Passing through isn't rude. Just sign "excuse me" as you go. You don't have to wait for a response. After all, they will want to get back to their chat!

Attention, Attention

To get the attention of someone at a distance, you can wave. The farther away the person is, the bigger your wave can be. If that person is really far away or out of your view, wave to someone between the two of you so he or she can get the person's attention for you. If someone isn't facing you, just tap his or her shoulder or upper arm. A few firm but gentle taps are fine.

A Brief History of Sign Language

Long before ASL was taught in classrooms, deaf people learned it from one another in their day-to-day interactions. ASL was passed from adult to child as well as from child to child. Formal teaching of ASL began in 1817 when an American, Thomas Hopkins Gallaudet, brought a deaf teacher named Laurent Clerc from France to the United States. Together they established the first American School for the Deaf in Hartford, Connecticut. Because of Laurent Clerc's influence, ASL and French Sign Language (FSL) are closely related. Many ASL and FSL sign words are similar.

Deaf Culture

ASL is one part of a rich deaf culture made up of shared experiences and traditions. You'll learn a little about deaf culture as you read this book. You'll learn lots more as you try out the signs you've learned with your deaf friends and classmates!

excuse me
With the fingers of one hand, draw two straight lines on the palm of the other.

hearing
Make a little circle in front of your mouth.

deaf
Touch your index finger to your ear and then to the side of your mouth.

Ready
With your fingers crossed, uncross your wrists and show your palms.

to sign?
Hand over hand, make a circle toward your chest.

yes!
Move your fist down and up— like it's nodding.

The Alphabet

A

B

C

D

E

F

G

H

I

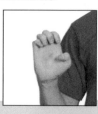
J

K

L

M

What is your name?

Put your palm out in the direction of the person.

Tap your bottom fingers with your top fingers.

Move your hands from side to side.

(your + name + what)

6

Make the first three letters of the alphabet around your spread fingers.

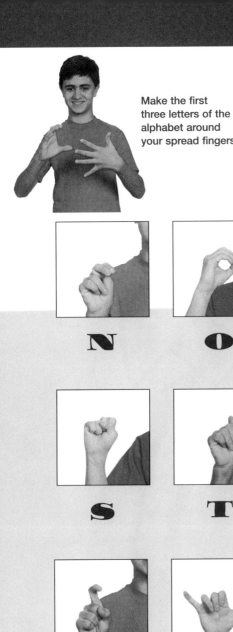

N O P Q R

S T U V W

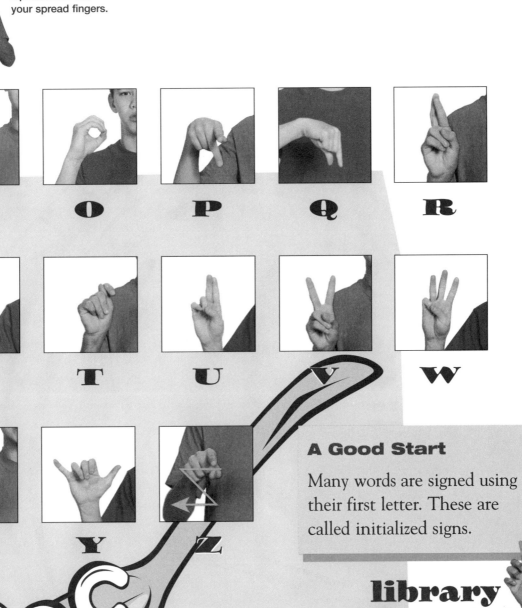

X Y Z

A Good Start

Many words are signed using their first letter. These are called initialized signs.

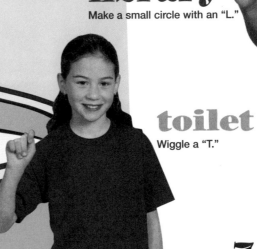

library
Make a small circle with an "L."

toilet
Wiggle a "T."

Numbers

Touch your fingertips, rotate your hands, and touch your fingers together again.

Flick your index finger twice.

Flick your fingers twice.

What time is it?

Touch your wrist with a questioning face.

tomorrow

Lay your thumb on your cheek and then move it forward, so that you can see it.

morning

Place one hand at the other elbow and bring your lower palm up toward your chin a little bit, as if the sun is starting to rise.

It's About Time!

yesterday

With your thumb on your cheek, rotate your hand so that your extended pinkie is back near your ear.

night

Cup your hand over your wrist.

today

Pull two "Y"s straight down.

day

Lay one arm down on top of the other.

Feelings and Emotions

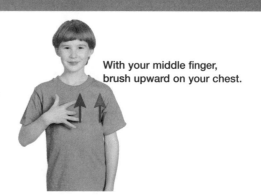

With your middle finger, brush upward on your chest.

Facial expressions are as crucial to signing as hand gestures and as natural as the faces you make every day. You can use the signs for "happy" or "sad" in conversation, but use your face to express yourself, too.

excited

With bent middle fingers, make alternating circles away from your chest.

angry

Make your hand into a claw. Starting at your chest, make an arc across your face.

love

Cross your wrists over your heart.

hate

Flick your middle fingers out and... open up your hands.

a. b.

SOLD OUT

Love Signals

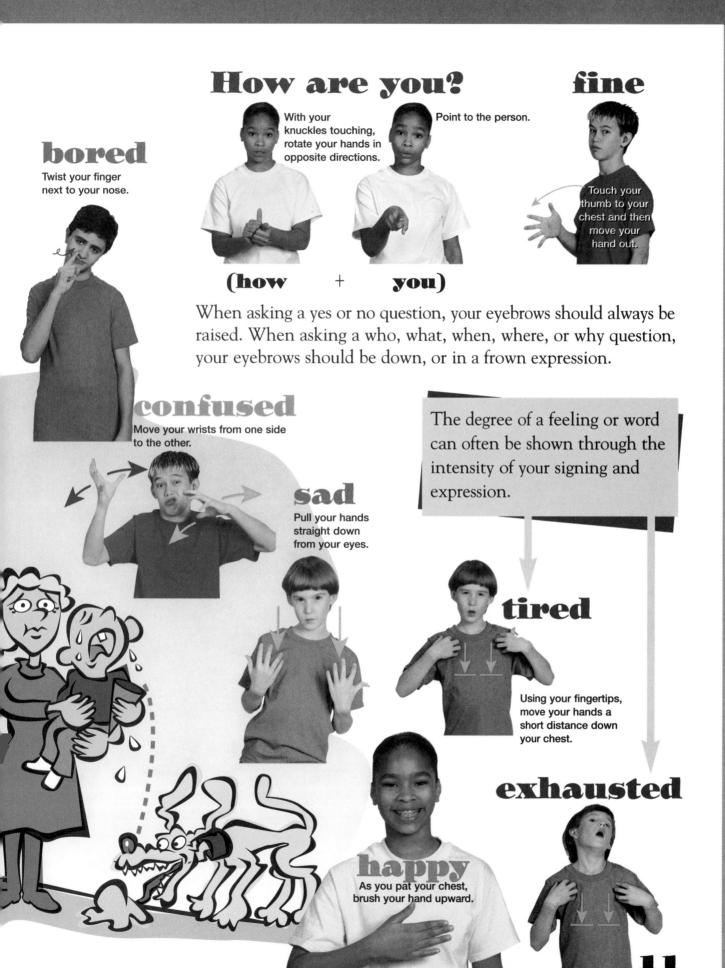

How are you?

bored
Twist your finger next to your nose.

With your knuckles touching, rotate your hands in opposite directions.

Point to the person.

(how + you)

fine
Touch your thumb to your chest and then move your hand out.

When asking a yes or no question, your eyebrows should always be raised. When asking a who, what, when, where, or why question, your eyebrows should be down, or in a frown expression.

confused
Move your wrists from one side to the other.

The degree of a feeling or word can often be shown through the intensity of your signing and expression.

sad
Pull your hands straight down from your eyes.

tired
Using your fingertips, move your hands a short distance down your chest.

exhausted

happy
As you pat your chest, brush your hand upward.

Calendar

Move a "C" hand up and over your other hand.

SUNDAY
Slide your hands down.

MONDAY
Make a tiny circle with an "M."

TUESDAY
Make a tiny circle with a "T."

WEDNESDAY
Make a tiny circle with a "W."

'Tis the Season

Winter/cold
Shiver as if you are cold.

Spring

a. With your fingers touching, move your hand behind the other hand and...

b. spread your fingers out as they emerge on the other side.

What are you doing tonight?

(this + night + you + do + what?)

Pull down two "Y"s.

Touch your index fingers to your thumbs.

SATURDAY
Make a tiny circle with an "S."

Make a tiny circle with an "H."

THURSDAY

Make a tiny circle with an "F."

FRIDAY

Summer
Draw your curved index finger across your forehead, as if you are wiping away sweat.

Autumn
Make a chopping motion at your elbow, as if a tree is being cut down.

Money

With your thumb and fingers touching as if you are holding cash, bring your hand down on your palm twice.

pay

Move your index finger out and away from your palm—like money flying out of your hand.

store/shop

Move your hands toward and away from your chest.

wallet

Put your palms together and then separate them, as if you're opening and closing a wallet.

buy

Pretend to lift money from your open palm and put it in front of you.

How much does the bicycle cost?

Pedal with your fists.

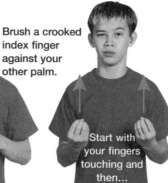
Brush a crooked index finger against your other palm.

Start with your fingers touching and then...

a.

open your hands and move them up toward your face.

b.

(bicycle   +   cost   +   how much?)

It Just Makes Cents!

dollars
Slide your right hand along the edge of your left hand.

cents
Move your index finger out from your forehead so you can see it.

Color

Wiggle your fingers on your chin.

green
Wiggle a "G."

pink
A "P" brushes down your chin.

purple
Tap a "P" down slightly.

orange
Squeeze your chin.

rainbow
Four fingers draw the shape of a rainbow in the air.

blue
Wiggle a "B."

What's your favorite?

Tap your middle finger on your chin.

(your + favorite + what?)

red
Move your index finger down your lips and chin.

yellow
Wiggle a "Y."

Seeing is believing

see
Touch the middle finger of your "V" hand to your eye and move it forward so that you can see it.

watch/look
Start with your fingers in the "see" position and then turn them around like two eyes watching.

white
Pull fingertips together and away from your chest.

a.   b.

Family

Two "F"s rotate around to face you.

a.   b.

mom
Touch your chin with your thumb.

grandfather
Touch your forehead with your thumb, then bring your hand down and extend it away from you.

grandmother
Touch your chin with your thumb, then bring your hand down and extend it away from you.

sister

Touch your chin with your thumb, then...

bring your hand down to sit on your wrist.

a.   b.

cousin
Wiggle a "C."

baby

Rock the baby!

I love you!

dad

Touch your forehead with your thumb.

Family

Did you notice that all the signs for female family members use the bottom half of the face and all the signs for male family members use the top half? This is because a long time ago, girls and women wore bonnets they tied beneath their chins and boys and men wore hats with brims.

brother

Touch your forehead with your thumb, then bring your hand down to sit on your wrist.

uncle

Make a tiny circle by the side of your head with a "U."

aunt

Make a tiny circle on your cheek with an "A."

19

People

Move "P"s in continuous circles away from your body.

tall
Put your hand above your head and look up at it.

woman
Put your thumb on your chin and bring your hand down to touch your chest.

girl
Run your thumb along your jaw.

young
With your fingertips, brush upward on your chest.

man
Put your thumb on your forehead and bring your hand down to touch your chest.

short
Put your hand at your hip.

boy
Tug the brim of a baseball cap.

Nice to meet you!

Run one palm down the length of the other.

(nice +

Bring two "D" hands together until your knuckles touch.

meet +

you)

Who said it's not polite to point!

It's easy to see that it's okay when you're signing. So pat yourself on the back. You're right on the nose!

eyes
Point to each eye.

nose
Point to your nose.

back
Pat your back.

old
Pull on your beard.

21

Clothes

Brush your
hands down
your chest.

shoes

Knock your
fists together.

pants

Pull up a pair of pants.

skirt

Move your hands
straight out
from hips.

KEEP OUT

shirt

Tug your shirt.

dirty

Put your hand
under your chin
and wiggle
your fingers.

Slide your index
fingers back
and forth.

socks

Who has my hat?

Put your hand flat on your chest.

Put your hand on your head.

Touch your chest with your fingertips.

Put your thumb on your chin and wiggle your index finger.

(my + hat + have + who?)

I'm signing in the rain!

raincoat (rain + coat)

With your fingers spread, throw your hands down twice, to imitate rain.

a.

b.

Run your thumbs down your chest.

umbrella

Put your fists together and then move the top one up, as if you are opening an umbrella.

boots

a.

Knock your fists together and...

b.

touch your hand to your wrist and then to your elbow.

23

Outside

a. With your fingers spread wide, pull your hand out from your other hand and...

b. close your fingers together.

moon
Look up at the moon.

cloud
Starting with your hands facing each other, move them from one side to the other—as if you're holding a cloud between them.

car
Grab the wheel.

home
Move your fingers from your mouth to your ear.

flower
Touch your hand under each side of your nose (as if you're smelling a flower).

24

sun

Make a fist and then open up your hand.

Pull two "L"s up.

Wiggle a "D."

(you + live + where)

Weather report

wind
Move your hands from side to side, as if they are blown by the wind.

snow
Your fingers become snowflakes that wiggle and float downward.

tree
Wiggle your hand like the leaves of a tree.

perfect
Your top fingers make a half circle and meet the bottom fingers with a tap.

hot
Move a clawed hand down and away from your mouth.

b.

warm
Brush your finger up and away from your mouth to show breath.

a.

Room

a.

b. Show the four sides of a box.

desk/table
With your palms facing down, bring your arms together.

chair
Sit two fingers of one hand on a chair you make with the fingers of your other hand. Now, pick up your top fingers and sit them down again.

KEEP OUT!

mirror
Look at yourself in a mirror you make with your hand.

light
a. Flick your chin with your middle finger and then...

b. make a fist and open it to show light coming down from above.

Do you want to come over?

Motion someone toward you.

Pull your hands toward you.

(come over + want)

bed
Lay your head down on the pillow you make with your hand.

private
Place your thumb over your lips and chin.

Knock Knock!
When your little brother or sister is at the door, these signs will come in handy.

Keep Out!
Making fists, cross your arms at the wrists.

alarm
Tap your palm with a "D."

27

Animals

With your fingertips on your chest, brush your hands toward each other twice.

rabbit

With your thumbs hooked together, bend your fingertips like twitching rabbit ears.

cat

Draw two cat's whiskers on your cheek.

dog

Snap your fingers twice.

snake

With bent "V" fingers, move your hand like a snake.

bird

With your thumb and index finger, make a bird's beak. Open and close it twice.

turtle

Cover your fist with your other palm and slide your thumb out to reveal the turtle's head.

28

I have a horse.

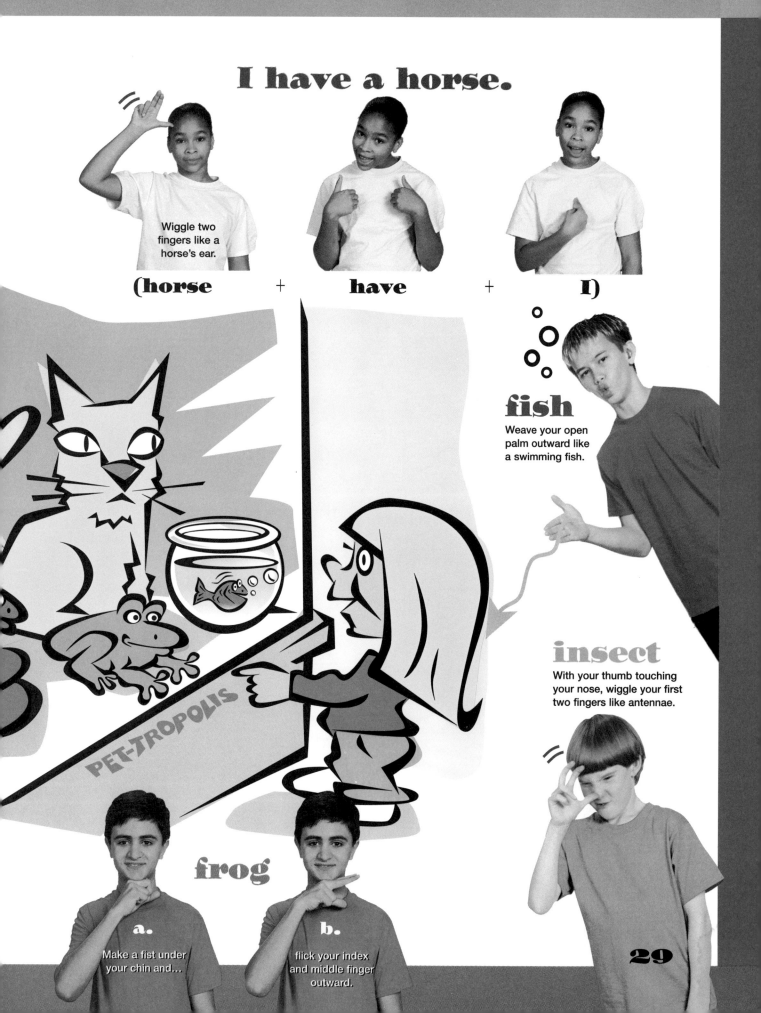

Wiggle two fingers like a horse's ear.

(horse + have + I)

fish
Weave your open palm outward like a swimming fish.

insect
With your thumb touching your nose, wiggle your first two fingers like antennae.

PET-TROPOLIS

frog

a.
Make a fist under your chin and…

b.
flick your index and middle finger outward.

29

Food

Touch your mouth twice.

drink

Bring a glass to your mouth and pretend to drink from it.

milk

Squeeze you fist and pretend to milk a cow!

sandwich

Make a sandwich with one hand around the other and pretend to eat it.

vegetable

Rotating your "V" hand, touch your index finger then your middle finger to the sides of your chin.

soda pop

a.

Making a fist, pull up...

b.

and pop your top hand on your bottom fist.

cookie

Rotate a circle on your palm.

30

Let's go to the cafeteria.

Point to yourself and the other person.

Point two hands in the direction of the cafeteria.

Follow the edge of your chin with a "C."

(you and I + go + cafeteria)

fruit
Give the letter "F" a little twist.

Time to eat!

hungry
Drag the letter "C" down your chest.

thirsty
Drag your index finger down you throat.

water
Tap a "W" on your chin twice.

Careers

Make fists and knock your wrists together.

Some careers and occupations have their own signs (dentist, doctor, police officer, nurse, fire fighter). But for many careers you sign the object or verb and add on the "agent" or "doer" sign (law + doer = lawyer, fly + doer = pilot, act + doer = actor).

dentist
With a bent index finger, touch your tooth.

agent/ doer sign
With your palms facing each other, move your hands straight down.

police officer
Place your index finger and thumb over your heart.

doctor
Take your pulse with a "D."

nurse
With an "N," tap your pulse.

fire fighter
Tuck in your thumb and put four fingers to your forehead.

BUS

I want to be an inventor.

With fingers spread and thumb tucked in, give a mini-salute.

Rotate your hands palm to palm.

(invent + doer sign + I + want + become)

lawyer

Slide an "L" down your palm.

a.

b.

c.

You Wanna Be a What?

Look in other parts of this book for the signs you may want to use. Such as art (page 40) + doer = artist, science (page 34) + doer = scientist, write (page 34) + doer = writer, dance (page 41) +doer = dancer, music (page 40) + doer = musician, photography + doer = photographer (page 41).

actor

Make fists with your thumbs extended and move your hands in circles away from your chest.

a.

b.

pilot

With your middle and ring fingers bent, move your hand through the air like a plane.

a.

b.

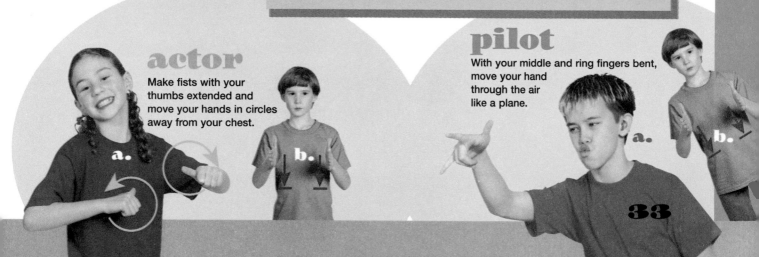

School

Pat your hands together.

class

Rotate two "C"s around until your hands meet and the "C"s face you.

read/reading

A "V" (like two eyeballs) reads up and down the page made by your other hand.

write

Pretend your index finger is your pen.

social studies

With an "S," make a small arc.

student

Pull your hand from your palm to your brain.

a. b.

(learn + doer sign)

English

Pull your hands slightly toward your chest.

book

Place your palms together, then open them like a book.

science

Pretend to pour something from two beakers.

I forgot my homework.

Knock your wrists together.

Wipe your palm across your forehead and...

close your hand into a fist.

	a.		b.		a.	b.
(My	**+**	**home**	**+**	**work**	**+**	**forgot)**

teacher

Pull the facts out of your brain!

(teach   +   doer sign)

Make the Grade

quiz/test
Draw question marks with your index fingers.

grades
Make a "G" on your hand.

math
Two "M"s motion up and brush each other at your wrists.

Sports

Put your fists together with your knuckles touching the heel of the opposite hand. Now rotate your fists back and forth.

skiing
Your hands are the skis.

football
Lace your fingers together.

swimming
Dog paddle with your hands.

gymnastics
Your upper hand rotates around your lower hand—just like a gymnast rotates around a bar.

skating
Move your hands forward and back.

a.

b.

Basketball is fun!

Put your hands in the air and flick your wrists twice.

With your first two fingers, strike the fingers of your other hand.

(basketball + fun)

soccer

Tap your bottom hand to your top hand twice.

Sports Talk

win

Swing one hand down and pretend to grab a trophy.

a.

b.

lose

Run a "V" across your wrist.

team

Make two "T"s. Circle them out and around until your little fingers meet.

a.

b.

baseball/softball

Hold your bat. Get ready to swing!

Action!

Move your hands from one side to the other.

jump
Use your fingers to jump off your palm.

run
Tug your front thumb with your back index finger.

walk
Step up and down with your hands.

throw
Pretend to throw something.

a.

b.

What do you want to play?

Move two "Y"s up, down, and back up again.

(you + want + play + what)

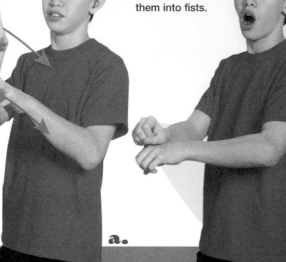

Gimme a Break!

nap/sleep

a. Start with your hand open and your palm facing you and then...

b. pull your hand away from your face and close the fingers together.

catch
Move both hands down and close them into fists.

rest
Cross your wrists and pull your hands toward your chest.

a.

b.

39

Interests

Pull your hands away from your chest and bring your thumbs and middle fingers together.

a. b.

music

Wave your hand in an 8 along your arm.

volunteer

Pull up on the back of your shirt.

travel

With curved fingers, make small loop-the-loops.

HOBBIES

art

Brush down your palm with your pinkie.

nature

Tap an "N" on your wrist.

I take dance lessons.

Swing your fingers back and forth on your palm.

Move your hand up and over on your palm, as if it's a turning page.

Pull your hands up and…

a.

close your fingers together.

b.

(dance + lessons + I + take up)

photography

Snap a photo.

It's all in Your Hands!

make

Knock your fists together, rotate them, and knock them together again.

build

Alternating one hand on top of the other, build up toward your chin.

41

Fun

With your first two fingers, strike the fingers of your other hand.

famous
Trace a big, curly mustache with your index fingers.

movie
Put one hand on the side of the other hand and move it from side to side.

stereo
Wiggle your hand by your ear.

Famous Movies

computer
Rub a "C" up and down your arm.

cartoons
Rub your nose twice with a "C."

Let's watch a video.

Make your fingers into two sets of eyes.

Circle a "V" on the palm of your other hand.

(you and I + watch + video)

magazine
Slide your fingers up and down on the edge of your hand.

On-line

Internet
With your middle fingers touching, rotate your hands in opposite directions.

web site
(Internet + setup)

With your thumb raised, put one fist on top of the other.

43

Conversation

Move your hands up and down.

friend

Index fingers lock together in friendship, then rotate and lock together again.

a.

b.

weird

Move a "C" across your face and down toward your shoulder.

a.

b.

cool

Touch your thumb to your chest and wiggle your fingers.

hearing aid

Hook your finger over your ear.

What's up?

With your middle fingers, draw an arch and end with your palms facing up.

good

Touch your hand on your mouth and then slap it on your palm.

because

Draw your index finger across your forehead.

why

Touch your forehead, then pull down a "Y."

a.

b.

See you later.

(see + later)

a. Make an "L" and...

b. point it down and away from you.

telephone

Pretend to talk on the phone.

It's for you!

To communicate by phone, many deaf people use a teletypewriter (TTY). Like a computer, this device has a screen and a keyboard. To call hearing people who do not have TTYs, deaf people use a telphone relay service where an operator using a TTY relays conversations. Most deaf people have a series of lights or vibrating beepers in their homes, which indicate anything from phone calls and door-bells to crying babies and oven timers.

remember

Bring the thumb at your forehead down to meet your other thumb.

okay

Sign an "O" and a "K" quickly.

a.

b.

Party

Using your wrists, swing two "P"s side to side.

candy

Twist your index finger on your cheek.

decorate/ decorations

Starting at shoulder height, put up decorations.

cake

Slice a cake with a "C" hand, going across your palm in each direction.

gift/ present

To give this gift, extend two "X"s out.

ice cream

Lick your ice cream cone.

When is your birthday?

 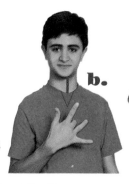

a. Touch your middle finger to your chin and move it down to your chest.

b.

Your top index finger makes a circle, then touches your bottom index finger.

(your + birthday + when)

How old are you?

(old + you)

Swift signs for Fast Food

pizza
Use a "P" to draw a large "Z" in the air.

french fries
With an "F," make a small arc.

hamburger
Make a pattie—one hand on top, then the other.

47

Index

goodbye!